THE BLUE DIESEL ERA

David Cable

Ian Allan PUBLISHING

First published 2014

ISBN 978 0 7110 3746 5

Published by Ian Allan Publishing Ltd, Hersham, Surrey KT12 4RG

Printed in Bulgaria

Visit the Ian Allan Publishing website at **www.ianallanpublishing.com**

Picture Credits
Every effort has been made to identify and correctly attribute photographic credits. Should any error have occurred this is entirely unintentional.

FRONT COVER A Class 27 heads west with a pair of three-car Class 101 DMUs at Saughton Junction in May 1986 (see page 22).

BACK COVER Power car No 43012 being seen bringing up the rear of a down train approaching Ruscombe in September of 1976 (see page 95).

TITLE PAGE No 107 432 prepares to depart North Berwick for Edinburgh with a healthy load in August 1987.

CONTENTS

Introduction

The blue era of British Railways can be said to have commenced with the unveiling in 1964 of the 'XP64' train, built to try out ideas for what would become the Mk 2 coach. The colour of the locomotive, No D1733, was slightly lighter than the shade eventually chosen for the full corporate image, introduced in 1965, when the system was re-branded as British Rail.

Prior to this date diesel locomotives were painted in green, main-line coaching stock in carmine and cream (known colloquially as 'blood and custard'), and other coaches in plain maroon, although Regional versions were applied, notably green on the Southern Region and chocolate and cream on the Western. The carmine-and-cream coaches eventually became maroon. Of course, many years passed before all the stock received the new colours.

The blue era saw the withdrawal of several of the first Modernisation Plan classes, some of which never received blue livery, and others only one or two representatives. Consequently, colour photographs of these examples are extremely rare. Some classes continued in work throughout the blue period and the sectorisation period whilst retaining blue livery. Some classes were enlarged and developed, some required replacement of below-standard diesel engines. The era heralded more-powerful locomotives as diesel engines were developed. Limited capacity at BR works initiated the building of BR locomotives overseas such as the Class 56s in Romania.

The InterCity 125 High Speed Train introduced the concept of fixed-formation main-line expresses, albeit with a power car at each end compared with the modern multi-powered coach units.

The colour scheme

The BR blue scheme adopted 'Monastral' blue as the basic colour, main-line coaching stock having a light-grey band surrounding the windows. Suburban coaches were plain blue, although with refurbishment (in some cases minimal), DMUs were repainted into blue and grey. However, some multiple-unit types, such as Classes 103 and 105, never received the blue-and-grey scheme, and nor did non-corridor stock or GUV-type vans.

The overall effect can best be described as bland.

Mandatory yellow ends were applied to the front of all locomotives and driving cabs, the yellow being carried round the cab side windows. The new BR double-arrow logo was introduced with this scheme, applied in white, as were locomotive and carriage-stock numbers.

When clean, the scheme could look tolerably attractive, but it deteriorated fairly quickly and, with brake and other dust, grease and oil spills, finished up in a miserable state. Younger generations who have seen this colour scheme only on well-maintained preserved rolling stock do not realise how well the introduction of the HST 'Flying Banana' scheme and the 'large logo' scheme for certain locomotive classes refreshed the old

network. The 'Banana' scheme took account of the shape of the nose of the HST power cars, and the yellow was extended halfway along the bottom of the body side, with the BR logo and 'Inter-City 125' in white in the upper half.

The 'large logo' scheme used on Classes 37, 47, 50 and 56 incorporated wraparound yellow ends extending back behind the cab doors, which had been pioneered on some Scottish Class 37s, with a full-height double-arrow logo and outsize numbers on the body side and pale-grey roof. This scheme looked particularly attractive on the larger locomotives such as Class 47s and, especially, Class 50s.

There were, of course, many variations, particularly on locomotives. Some had large logos with small numbers or vice versa, Stratford depot pioneered silver roofs with the basic scheme on some Class 31s and 47s, plus the odd DMU cab, Union Jack flags were applied to two Class 47s to celebrate HM The Queen's Silver Jubilee, a few Class 33s were given grey or silver roofs, some Class 50s in 'large logo' colours had black instead of grey roofs, and one had a blue roof. Some refurbished DMUs of Classes 101, 108 and 117/118 appeared in a reverse livery of very pale grey with a blue stripe, and a similar scheme was used for Pullman stock and the prototype HST.

Various white stripes and white cab window surrounds also appeared on some examples of Classes 31, 33, 37 and 55. Thornaby depot applied red solebars to some Class 20s, and a Class 47 (No 47 361) had a yellow band painted across the bottom of the bodyside. There were also other odd items such as the APT-P, Class 101 'Stourton Special', Class 25 No 25 322, Class 33 No 33 019, Class 47 No 47 583 and Class 37 No 37 093, which was painted in Police colours for advertising purposes.

Almost every class on the system carried the corporate colours, (noteworthy exceptions being Classes 01 and 02), although some had only one or two representatives. The Class 22s have been excluded since they have been covered comprehensively in the Ian Allan publication *Hydraulics in the West.*

A complete breakaway from the blue scheme was made in the mid-1980s with the introduction of the InterCity, Railfreight and Provincial sector colours, although it was an appreciable time before the blue schemes finally disappeared.

Spread of operations

Compared with the situation that developed under sectorisation and privatisation, the major classes of locomotives and multiple-units were less restricted in their areas of operation, apart of course from those lines which had axle-loading restrictions.

The locomotive classes which originated from the 1955 Modernisation Plan and which were built only in small quantities tended to be limited to certain areas in their last days. The 'D6xx' 'Warships' in Cornwall, the Class 28 Co-Bos in the Furness area and the 'Baby Deltics' on the GN London-area lines come to mind among types that hardly ventured away from their final operating territories. However, the principal classes had a very wide range of operating areas, and some examples are listed below:

Class 08	Throughout Britain wherever there were yards and sidings
Class 17	Midlands, North of England and Scottish Central Belt
Class 20	Primarily Midlands, North of England and Scottish Central Belt
Class 25	Broadly west of a line from Weymouth to Norwich
Class 31	Most areas apart from Southern Region (except Bristol–Portsmouth) and Scotland
Class 33	Principally Southern Region, but also for a period on Crewe–Cardiff services
Class 37	Throughout Britain except Southern Region (apart from Ripple Lane–Micheldever)
Class 40	Generally the North of England
Class 45	Midland main line south of Leeds; also Trans-Pennine
Class 46	Services from the North East to Liverpool and to the South West of England
Class 47	Universal within axle-load limits
Class 50	Initially on the West Coast main line north of Crewe, later on Great Western and South Western main lines
Class 52	Western Region only
Class 55	Initially confined to the East Coast main line but latterly on Newcastle–Liverpool trains
Class 56	Throughout England and South Wales where heavy industry, coal and construction requirements existed

Class 101	Mainly Eastern England and Scotland
Class 108	Midlands and Northern England
Class 114	Lincolnshire
Class 115	Chiltern lines
Classes 116-8	Bristol/Birmingham, WR London area and South Wales/South West England respectively
Class 120	Western Midlands including Nottingham area, and South Wales
Classes 123/4	Trans-Pennine services, notably serving Hull and Scarborough
Class 127	Midland main line (London area)

Class 201-3	Hastings line
Class 205-7	Non-electrified Southern Region lines

Classes 253/4 Initially Great Western and East Coast main lines, later on NE–SW services and Midland main line

These descriptions are not exhaustive but indicate where the observer might reasonably have expected to see representatives of these classes in the blue era.

Variety of classes

At the outset of the blue era the number of classes that could be seen was extensive, even ignoring instance where types were reclassified because of re-engining or re-gearing, such as with Classes 08/09, 21/29, 30/31 and 47/48.

The totals of each type (approximate due to some grouping of similar types such as Classes 201-203) are shown below with the number at the start and end of the blue era, having taken account of new types introduced during the era, and for comparison, the number working in the current era of privatisation. The latter shows classes seen in regular use and excludes classes which have been preserved on private lines. Some classes in 2013 have only a handful of locomotives working on the main line, such as Classes 31 and 56.

	1966	1985	2013
Locomotives	36	16	12
DMU/DEMUs	28	23	19
Total	64	39	31

This reinforces the long-held belief that in the old days there was much more variety, and the loss of locomotive classes is dramatically demonstrated. Whereas once there was variety of classes and monotony of colour, we now have far fewer classes but much more colour.

Photographs

Unless credited individually, photographs are of my own taking and on the whole are previously unpublished, although a number have been available from Colour-Rail. Unfortunately space constraints have rendered it impossible to show every class in every colour scheme, although I have striven to include a representative selection. On the other hand, certain classes seem seldom to have been recorded in BR blue at all, for various reasons – certain photographers generally were still using black-and-white film, those that were using colour didn't visit the requisite areas, and still others just weren't interested in non-steam trains.

For some inexplicable reason, for a period during the mid-1970s I failed to record locomotive numbers or train workings, and I apologise for their omission.

My thanks go to those photographers who have kindly supplied pictures for inclusion in this book, and also to the staff of Ian Allan Publishing. In addition there are individuals of whom special mention must be made, firstly my good friend Wally Stamper, whose patience in trying to render old, deteriorating slides suitable for publication has been very much appreciated, and secondly, Paul Cripps did an excellent job researching some obscure facts.

David Cable
Hartley Wintney
September 2013

CHAPTER 1 SHUNTERS

ABOVE Class 03 station pilot No 03 063 and its match wagon await custom at Newcastle Central in May 1984.

TOP The snowplough dwarfs Class 03 No 03 119 on shed at Landore in August 1977. One wonders whether, besides pushing the plough, the locomotive would have any strength to clear any snow!

ABOVE The last member of Class 05 remaining in BR stock, No 05 001, stands engaged on departmental duties, occupying the bay platform at Sandown on the Isle of Wight, in June 1976. It was subsequently replaced by a Class 03.

TOP A most unexpected arrival in the South East in 1981 was a lone example of Class 06, a type hitherto confined to the Scottish Region. No 06 003 was transferred to work at Reading Signal Works, being seen at Reading depot in May. Note that the coupling rods had been removed for towing south; in those days such transfers were effected by rail, not road. The locomotive would later be renumbered 97 804. A second locomotive was transferred a few months later.

ABOVE The Class 07 shunters spent their working lives in and around Southampton Docks. No 07 010 is seen at Eastleigh in March 1978 at the end of a line Class 74 electro-diesels doomed for the scrapheap. No 07 010 survived and is now on Avon Valley Railway.

TOP An unidentified Class 08 shunts the yard at Dringhouses, south of York, in April 1986. Apart from the through running lines, everything in this picture has since disappeared, and, after a period when open land allowed photography on the up side, a housing estate now occupies the site of the yard.

ABOVE Class 08 No 08 650 shunts the Freightliner wagon workshop yard at Southampton in September 1987. The construction of the wagon chassis is clearly apparent.

FACING PAGE TOP In the 1980s several depots embellished their Class 08 shunters. Complete with unofficial name, yellow cab window surrounds and silver roof, No 08 641 stands on shed at Laira in December 1987.

FACING PAGE BOTTOM No 08 935 hauls a train of coal hoppers from Westbury yard into the cement works in January 1988.

THIS PAGE TOP At the north end of Carlisle station an unidentified Class 08 shunts the stock of a train from Glasgow via the Glasgow & South Western in February 1988.

THIS PAGE CENTRE Portrait of Class 09 No 09 004 ex works at Eastleigh in April 1983 – a time when, having sought permission from the shed foreman, one could wander around the depot without any restrictions. The Class 09 was a higher-geared version of the Class 08 especially for Southern Region duties.

THIS PAGE BOTTOM The three Class 13s were formed from pairs of Class 08s (one with cab removed) coupled permanently. No 13 003 was photographed at Tinsley yard in June 1984. Not surprisingly they were known as 'master & slave' units. *Gavin Morrison*

CHAPTER 2 TYPE 1s

ABOVE One of the short-lived Class 17s, No D8542, enters Motherwell with an up freight in March 1968. *Jim Binnie*

TOP Another Class 17, No D8583, heads an Alloa–Motherwell freight through Larbert in August 1970. *Jim Binnie*

ABOVE Bringing a short coal train along the line from Ayr, a pair of Class 20s, No 20 125 leading, approach Elderslie Junction in September 1979.

ABOVE Pinxton signalbox stands guard as No 20 119 and a classmate pass with a train of empties returning to one of the East Midlands collieries in March 1986.

BELOW Class 20s Nos 20 043 and 20 093 approach Mexborough in August 1988 with a train of steel billets. In the background, forking away to the right, is the line to Wath.

LEFT Headed by a pair of Class 20s, No 20 043 leading, a train of steel-coil empties snakes its way past the east end of Tinsley yard in February 1988.

BELOW In the mid-1980s Thornaby depot enhanced some of its Class 20s with red solebars and applied unofficial names. Thus adorned, Nos 20 172 *Redmire* and 20 028 *Bedale* pass through Thornaby station with a Redmire–Redcar limestone train in February 1988.

CHAPTER 3 TYPE 2s

ABOVE Class 31/4 No 31 404, with white bodyside stripe as applied by Finsbury Park depot, rounds the curve at Southcote Junction with an up van train, probably from Plymouth, in July 1981.

RIGHT Class 23 'Baby Deltic' No D5909, seen stabled at King's Cross in July 1969, was the only example of its class to be painted in blue livery. *David Percival*

CENTRE LEFT Class 24 No 5096 propels a brake van near Polmont in November 1973.

CENTRE RIGHT Class 24s Nos D5132 and D5113 storm under a bridge near Plean in November 1973, on their way from Edinburgh to Inverness. Note the special headlights.

BOTTOM Lined up at Manchester Victoria in June 1974 are, from left to right, a Class 104 at the platform which led through to Manchester Exchange (the longest in the UK at one time), a Class 24 which was available for banking trains up to Newton Heath, a Class 124 Trans-Pennine DMU and a Class 110 DMU. Note also the maroon station nameboard, redolent of a past era.

THIS PAGE TOP Class 24s No 24 069 and 24 070 stand at the end of a line of withdrawn locomotives at Haymarket shed in August 1975.

THIS PAGE CENTRE No 24 023 wends its way between Bescot station and shed in October 1975.

THIS PAGE BOTTOM Pictured on the up through road at Hereford, No 25 054 stands at the head of a northbound mixed freight in April 1984. The DMU at the platform will take precedence.

FACING PAGE TOP Looking for all the world like a model, a short departmental train headed by a Class 25 makes its way south near Madeley in June 1984.

FACING PAGE CENTRE Having started from Wolverhampton behind Class 50 No 50 050 *Fearless*, the 'Coastway Crusader' railtour of 27 July 1986 travelled to Littlehampton via Bristol and Westbury, and included in the itinerary was a run down the Ludgershall branch behind Class 25s Nos 25 191 and 25 181, which had taken over at Bristol from Class 45/1 No 45 128. Already recorded in the Wylye Valley and at Grateley, the train was photographed again at Andover, where, shortly after this shot was taken, No 25 181 was declared a failure and replaced by Class 33 No 33 011. Note that by now InterCity-liveried stock was becoming more widespread.

FACING PAGE BOTTOM Class 25 No 25 199 shunts the yard at Watford Junction in September 1986.

FACING PAGE TOP Class 26/1 No 26 035, sporting a full set of headcode discs, snowploughs and extra headlights (used for some Scottish workings), is posed in the sun outside Eastfield shed in July 1982.

FACING PAGE CENTRE The 150th anniversary of the Great Western Railway, in 1985, was marked by a number of depot open days, one of which was held at Westbury in May. Among the exhibits was Class 25 No 25 322, which had a modified blue colour scheme with black logos in a swept round yellow front end and was unofficially named 'Tamworth Castle'.

FACING PAGE BOTTOM Another view of No 26 035, recorded three years later, working an eastbound train of empty Cartics past Saughton Junction on a murky day in March 1985. Note that the locomotive is now devoid of its discs, lights and snowploughs.

THIS PAGE TOP An unidentified Class 26 brings a short rake of ballast wagons past the signalbox at Perth station on a dull day in March 1988.

THIS PAGE CENTRE Class 27 No D5355 brings its Oban–Glasgow Queen Street train through Glen Falloch on a overcast day in January 1974.

THIS PAGE BOTTOM In the 1970s Glasgow–Edinburgh services were normally worked by pairs of Class 27s topping-and-tailing six-coach rakes of Mk 2 stock, until replaced by Class 47/7s operating with push-pull sets. Class 27s Nos D5413 and D5400 are seen near Linlithgow with an afternoon train for Edinburgh in October 1973.

FACING PAGE TOP Class 27/2 No 27 210 tails the 11.30 train for Edinburgh, seen departing Glasgow Queen Street on time in August 1975. Full power will be needed for the climb up to Cowlairs.

FACING PAGE BOTTOM A Class 27 heads west with a pair of three-car Class 101 DMUs at Saughton Junction in May 1986. The reason for this unusual combination is unknown, but the presence of passengers in the train suggests a mechanical failure of some sort.

THIS PAGE TOP Photographed in May 1987 at the west end of Dundee station, No 27 025 heads a short freight comprising an interesting mix of wagon types.

THIS PAGE CENTRE A Class 27 heads through Irvine with southbound coal empties on a foul day in March 1987.

THIS PAGE BOTTOM Class 28 Co-Bo No D5701 heads away from the camera with a Whitehaven–Heysham Moss tank train near Grange-over-Sands in June 1968. This locomotive was the only one of its class to receive BR blue livery. *Michael Mensing*

THIS PAGE TOP Recently rebuilt from a Class 21, Class 29 No D6107 is pictured at Larbert in June 1967, having failed in charge of a train from Aberdeen to Glasgow Queen Street. Replacement motive power would materialise in the form of Class 20 No D8118. *Jim Binnie*

THIS PAGE CENTRE Class 29 No 6124 approaches Carmuirs East Junction with a down freight for Grangemouth in May 1971. *Jim Binnie*

THIS PAGE BOTTOM Class 31s were a common sight throughout much of England. In this view, recorded in May 1975, an early 'skinhead' version is heading north between Saunderton and Princes Risborough, at the point where the up and down lines separate. The load is predominantly coal, probably for the cement works at Chinnor.

FACING PAGE TOP Exeter St Davids in August 1981, when semaphores abounded and trains to Barnstaple were still locomotive-hauled. The unidentified Class 31 has charge of a train of five coaches – rather more than are provided for today's travellers.

FACING PAGE BOTTOM Class 31/4 No 31 430 pulls away from Kirkby Stephen on a crisp day in February 1985 with a Leeds–Carlisle service – one of only a few then being provided between the two cities.

THIS PAGE TOP Class 31/1 No 31 221 heads a long rake of empties towards Horbury Junction in August 1988.

THIS PAGE CENTRE A grubby Class 31/1, No 31 292, shunts the Blue Circle Cement (BCC) depot at Handsworth in January 1988. The depot was at the end of a spur from Smethwick West station that had originally formed part the GWR main line between Birmingham and Wolverhampton.

THIS PAGE BOTTOM Nicely lit by late-afternoon sun in August 1983, a Class 31 comes off the line from Bury St Edmunds to join the Great Eastern main line at Haughley Junction with a train from Peterborough to Harwich.

FACING PAGE TOP Class 31/4s were standard fare on the Hope Valley line in August 1986; here No 31 438 charges past the entrance to Earle's Sidings with a Cleethorpes–Liverpool train. Note the signalman on his toes, setting the home signal to Danger.

FACING PAGE BOTTOM Seen from the signalbox at Manton Junction in February 1987, one of the silver-roofed Class 31s, No 31 416, exits the tunnel and takes the line to East Anglia with a Birmingham–Norwich train. By now locomotives were being fitted with a high-intensity headlight on each cab front – a worthwhile addition on a filthy example such as this.

CHAPTER 4 TYPE 3s

ABOVE The classic view at Worting Junction, with a Class 33/1 in charge of a VSOE special from Victoria to Bournemouth in September 1987.

ABOVE A favourite haunt for Class 33s was the Wylye Valley. Here late-winter sunshine illuminates a Portsmouth Harbour–Cardiff train at Sherrington in February 1988.

RIGHT A Portsmouth Harbour–Bristol train, with Class 33/0 in charge, descends the bank from Upton Scudamore and passes the up platform at Dilton March in July 1983. The standard lamp looks completely out of character with the very basic station.

BELOW A most unusual working, recorded in May 1984 at the foot crossing just west of Battledown Flyover. No 33 001 was heading east with an exhibition train, the well wagon behind the locomotive carrying narrow-gauge 0-4-2T *Talyllyn*.

THIS PAGE TOP Ludgershall in July 1984, with No 33 027 *Earl Mountbatten of Burma* about to depart with an MoD train for Eastleigh. Note the MoD shunter on the right. The sidings here have been much reduced since the photograph was taken.

THIS PAGE CENTRE Class 33s were allocated to work Crewe/Manchester–Cardiff services for a period in the early 1980s. Here a Crewe-bound train is seen passing the site of the old station at Woofferton in June 1984.

THIS PAGE BOTTOM Four Class 33s were painted with white window surrounds. Here '33/1' No 33 101 approaches Salisbury Tunnel Junction with a Waterloo–Salisbury train formed of a pair of '4-TC' trailer units in August 1983. Judging from the exhaust, it must have been checked for a Romsey-line train.

FACING PAGE TOP One Class 33/0, No 33 012, was painted in livery similar to the 'large logo' scheme but without the full-size characters. This lasted for less than a year, before the authorities insisted the locomotive be returned to standard livery – a great pity, as the non-standard scheme appeared to be a considerable improvement. It is seen here at Woking, presumably having failed, in March 1982, being towed east by Class 73/1 electro-diesel No 73 124.

FACING PAGE CENTRE In the late 1980s, when the Class 442 'Wessex Electrics' were being built (using motors from the outgoing '4-REP' units), fast trains between Waterloo and Bournemouth were generally powered by Class 73s electro-diesels, but in this most unusual view, recorded at Millbrook in September 1987, a Class 33 is propelling a Waterloo–Bournemouth service of '5-TC' and '4-TC' stock.

FACING PAGE TOP In December 1987 No 33 056 *The Burma Star* was seen with a pair of thin white bodyside stripes, being pictured thus at Southampton Central in charge of a Portsmouth Harbour–Bristol train.

FACING PAGE BOTTOM A familiar scene at Wokingham, here featuring a pair of Class 33s taking the Ascot road with a train of empties on their way back from Theale depot to the BCC works at Northfleet, in June 1987. The wagons are double-bodied bogie versions of the standard PCA.

THIS PAGE TOP In May 1988 a Waterloo–Meldon special double-headed by a pair of Class 33s traversed the Portsmouth Direct line. Complete with headboard and white marker discs, No 33 112 *Templecombe* accelerates the train away from the Haslemere stop.

THIS PAGE BELOW In March 1988 an enthusiasts' special visited various branch lines along the Hampshire and Dorset coasts, the train being formed of a pair of '4-TC' units powered by Class 33/1 No 33 103. Having visited Lymington, it is seen here making its way through typical New Forest scenery as it heads back to Brockenhurst, on a line seldom used by locomotives.

TOP Silver-roofed Class 33/0 No 33 025 crosses the River Hamble at Bursledon in April 1984, with a Portsmouth Harbour– Bristol train.

CENTRE Not all of the Class 35 'Hymeks' were painted in BR blue, but among those so treated was No 7029, seen here in March 1974 entering Sonning Cutting with a good selection of the types of wagon that used to form vacuum-braked freight trains.

BOTTOM Passing the gantry guarding the branch at Manuel Junction, Class 37 No D6904 heads east with a load of tanks from Grangemouth refinery in January 1974.

TOP Over the years a variety of motive power could be seen hauling iron-ore trains from Port Talbot to Llanwern, including Class 56s and Mendip-based Class 59s. But for sheer impact, both visual and aural, nothing surpassed the triple-heading Class 37s used in the 1970s; here three truly filthy examples are seen rounding the curve from Bridgend station in February 1976.

CENTRE The Welsh Class 37s undertook all sorts of duties, both passenger and freight. An example of a local trip working is shown passing Whitland in October 1976. The days of full headcodes have gone, and four zeros will in time be replaced with two marker lights. The four Presflos are probably destined for the cement works at Aberthaw.

BOTTOM For many years following the demise of steam, Class 37s were standard fare on main-line services in East Anglia. This example is seen near Sawston, working a King's Lynn–Liverpool Street express, in April 1977.

LEFT A pair of Class 37s approach Chesterfield with the daily Lackenby–Corby steel coils in October 1985. At around this time Thornaby depot embellished a number of locomotives with white stripes and the depot's kingfisher emblem, among them this pair, Nos 37 062 *British Steel Corby* and 37 078 *Teesside Steelmaster*.

BELOW Photographed from the signalbox at Shirebrook in May 1986, Class 37 No 37 203 heads north towards Elmton & Cresswell with a train of merry-go-round empties.

TOP The era of sectorisation might be upon us, but BR blue and locomotive haulage still hold sway at Inverness in May 1987, as Class 37/4s Nos 37 417 *Highland Region* and 37 421, both in 'large logo' livery with Inverness depot's Highland Stag motif, await departure for Thurso and Wick.

ABOVE 'Large logo' Class 37 No 37 175 ambles through Plymouth with a train of clay hoods from Marsh Mills via Tavistock Junction to Carne Point in June 1987.

THIS PAGE TOP Autumn mist hangs in the air near Stanhope in November 1987 as No 37 128 makes its way up the branch towards the Weardale Cement Works at Eastgate (since closed) with empties from Tyne Yard.

THIS PAGE CENTRE In charge of a train of oil tanks from the BP refinery at Grangemouth, a pair of Class 37s pass the ex-Caledonian Railway signalbox at Fouldubs Junction in March 1988. Note the bow window, which was full of tomato plants!

THIS PAGE BOTTOM Comprising a wonderful array of wagons, a Class 37-powered Speedlink service takes the line to Mossend at Greenhill Lower Junction in March 1988.

FACING PAGE TOP A pair of Class 37s bring a train of empty iron-ore hoppers past Melton Ross en route from Frodingham to Immingham in July 1987.

FACING PAGE BOTTOM With a puff of smoke No 37 146 leaves the BCC terminal at Middlesbrough for Tees Yard in February 1988 with empties for onward transit to Tyne Yard, where they will join up with the empties from the BCC depot at Heaton terminal for return to Eastgate. Note the basic large logo features of yellow cab and large number, but a small BR logo.

CHAPTER 5 TYPE 4s

ABOVE Class 40 No 40 010 awaits departure from Glasgow Central with an express working (judging from the headcode discs), possibly to Carlisle via the GSWR line, in September 1979.

TOP No 40 080 heads south at Chaloner's Whin with a short parcels train in May 1980.

CENTRE A freight comprising a good mixture of wagons passes Tollerton behind an unidentified Class 40 in May 1980.

BOTTOM From the opposite direction, an earlier-built Class 40, by now devoid of its headcode discs, heads north with more freight traffic.

TOP The hills are alive with the sound of a pair of Class 40s arriving at Peak Forest with a train of Peakstone hoppers (which hardly justifies the express headcode!) in February 1983. Nos 40 104 and 40 141 would retire to Buxton shed later in the day.

CENTRE A split-headcode Class 40 makes its way south past Dorrington with a train of tank wagons in April 1984. Note that the signalman has been prompt in setting the signal to Danger, in line with traditional Great Western practice.

BOTTOM Two of the original 'Warships', latterly designated Class 41, gained blue livery, these being Nos D600 and D602. No D600 *Active* is pictured on shed at Laira in June 1967. *David Percival*

TOP One of the Class 42 'Warships', No 810 *Cockade*, heads a mixed freight, probably from Feltham, near Wandsworth Road in September 1970. Judging from the sky, the photographer is about to be soaked! *Harry Luff*

CENTRE Class 42 'Warship' No 806 *Cambrian* passes Winchfield in June 1972 with a Merstham–Westbury train of stone empties, having made a delivery for building part of the M25. The land in the background is now occupied by a housing estate, whose residents no doubt complain about the noise of the trains!

BOTTOM Class 43 'Warship' No 851 *Temeraire* brings a Sunday Treherbert–Margate excursion past Midgham c1970. Is this the train taken by the apocryphal couple from Margate who went on holiday to South Wales, caught a mystery excursion and, finding themselves in Margate, went home, had a cup of tea and did a bit of work in the garden before returning to their holiday hotel? *David Canning*

THIS PAGE TOP Class 44 'Peak' No 44 004, by this time unnamed, heads towards the tunnel near Alfreton with a northbound mixed freight comprising a goodly selection of vehicles; once again, the headcode discs are incorrect for the type of train. The date is October 1978, and the original four-track main line has been halved.

THIS PAGE CENTRE In July 1975, when Class 45s enjoyed a monopoly of express workings on the Midland main line, a split-headcode example passes the gasometers on the approach to St Pancras, at the end of its journey from Leeds. Note the man off the end of the platform, almost invisible in his dark clothing – justification, if any were needed, of why 'high-visibility' jackets are now mandatory.

THIS PAGE BOTTOM In their later years Class 45s were commonplace on Trans-Pennine workings. Here a Newcastle–Liverpool express prepares to stop at Northallerton in June 1981.

FACING PAGE TOP Class 45s could also be found in North Wales, as apparent from this photograph of a Scarborough–Llandudno train calling at Flint on a murky day in March 1984. The steam heating was doubtless very welcome.

FACING PAGE CENTRE Heading a train of PCV tankers bound for the BCC depot at Northenden, a Class 45 emerges from a full yard at Earles Sidings in May 1985.

FACING PAGE BOTTOM Working a Bristol–Taunton stopping service in June 1985, a Class 45 passes the splendid array of signals controlling the approach to Taunton.

FACING PAGE TOP Severn Tunnel Junction in April 1986, with a Class 45 and its train clattering over the points on the approach to the tunnel.

FACING PAGE CENTRE An interesting pairing hauls the unloaded coal hoppers off the loop alongside the cooling towers at Didcot power station in May 1986. The locomotives are Class 45/0 No 45 062 and Class 58 No 58 001, the latter having presumably experienced some problem further north.

FACING PAGE BOTTOM A Class 45 approaches Rotherham Masborough in June 1987, returning to Earles Sidings with the empties (seemingly an unusually large number on that day) from Dewsbury cement depot.

THIS PAGE TOP Once upon a time one could drive up the M5/M6 past Bescot, see what was stabled near the station, and if there was anything of interest, turn off at Junction 9 for the station and footpath alongside the sidings. In July 1987 your author spotted No 45 107 bearing one of Tinsley's unofficial names, 'Phoenix'.

THIS PAGE CENTRE Class 46 No 46 029 accelerates past Briton Ferry in August 1977 with a Freightliner service from Danygraig, of rather curious make-up.

THIS PAGE BOTTOM A Gateshead-allocated Class 46 speeds past the crossing near Muskham with a northbound parcels train in June 1980.

THIS PAGE TOP Only one Class 46 was ever named. Displaying the regimental crest above its nameplate, No 46 026 *Leicestershire and Derbyshire Yeomanry* comes off shed at Toton in June 1983.

THIS PAGE CENTRE An inter-regional express headed by a Class 47 passes Mortimer church northbound in June 1983. Unfortunately the locomotive was not identifiable – unlike the nearest cow!

THIS PAGE BOTTOM Class 47/4 No 47 572 is working hard as it approaches Haughley Junction with the down 'East Anglian' late on a sunny afternoon in August 1983.

FACING PAGE TOP The semaphore at Marchwood is 'off' for a tank train from Fawley refinery heading for Totton and the main line in June 1984. In charge is a rather work-stained Class 47/0, No 47 290.

FACING PAGE CENTRE King's Lynn Junction signalbox looms over an express nearing the end of its journey from Liverpool Street in August 1986 behind Class 47/4 No 47 579 *James Nightall G.C.*, with Stratford depot's trademark silver roof. On the left is the branch to Middleton Towers.

FACING PAGE BOTTOM The driver of the unique Class 47/9 No 47 901 applies full throttle to help a stone train from Whatley out of Westbury and up the bank to Upton Scudamore. This was the locomotive used as an engine testbed in advance of the introduction of the Class 58 Type 5 design. Note the non-standard lamp clusters.

FACING PAGE TOP No 47 212 passes Bedford station one Saturday morning in March 1988 with the empty tanks from Langley to Lindsey.

FACING PAGE BOTTOM Comprising no fewer than 16 coaches, of Mk 1 and Mk 3 design, the magnificent 'Highland Tour Train' passes Ouston Junction, south of Newcastle, in June 1988 – just as the electrification masts were being erected. In charge is 'large logo' Class 47/4 No 47 650, complete with Eastfield depot's Highland Terrier motif, which also appears on the train headboard.

THIS PAGE TOP Class 47/4 No 47 586 in a 'halfway house' livery, with wraparound yellow ends (complete with 'Highland Rail' stag motif) but minus the large logo and numerals. It was photographed in charge of an Aberdeen–Inverness service at Elgin in May 1987, by which time an complete rake of Mk 2 stock still in Rail blue and grey was becoming a rarity.

THIS PAGE CENTRE On the occasion of its open day in July 1981 Stratford depot was thronged with visitors, to the extent that obtaining a picture without them was near-impossible; at least the small boy clambering into the cab of an immaculate No 47 583 *County of Hertfordshire* blends in with the front bogie! This special version of 'large logo' livery had been applied to celebrate the forthcoming wedding of HRH The Prince of Wales and Lady Diana Spencer and would later be modified with the addition of red and blue panels within the horizontal stripes.

THIS PAGE BOTTOM In charge of the overnight sleeper from King's Cross to Aberdeen, 'large logo' Class 47/4 No 47 664 passes the Blue Circle depot at Craiginches early one morning in May 1987.

FACING PAGE TOP Photographed from the top of the cement silo at BCC's Kidlington depot, a Southampton-bound Freightliner heads south behind an unidentified Class 47 in July 1987.

FACING PAGE BOTTOM Headed by '47/4' No 47 522, an Ascot race-day special rounds the curve into Wokingham as it heads back north with a full load of satisfied customers (or perhaps not, if they had lost out to the bookies!) in July 1987.

THIS PAGE TOP No 47 457 *Ben Line* heads east through the centre of Manchester Victoria with an interesting mix of parcels vans in July 1987. The exhaust plume reveals that the driver has opened the regulator for the climb to Miles Platting.

THIS PAGE BOTTOM Headed by Class 47/4 No 47 638 *County of Kent*, the Plymouth–Brighton express passes through Woolston station in September 1987, with the Itchen road bridge dominating the background.

FACING PAGE TOP Comprising a rake of largely Mk 2 stock in Provincial Sector colours but hauled by a Class 47/4 still in Rail blue, a Newcastle–Liverpool express passes Ravensthorpe in February 1988. Note the nothbound working disappearing in the background.

FACING PAGE BOTTOM Rounding the curve at Carlisle South Junction, Class 47/4 No 47 441 heads for the Settle–Carlisle line on its way to Leeds in February 1988.

THIS PAGE TOP Complete with miniature snowploughs and Highland Terrier motif, Class 47/0 No 47 118 leaves the Blue Circle works at Oxwellmains in August 1987 with a train of PCA tankers destined for the depots at Dundee East and Craiginches. This was one of five Brush Type 4 locomotives fitted originally with a V-form Sulzer engine and as such was initially desginated Class 48 under TOPS.

THIS PAGE CENTRE An unidentified Class 50 heads a southbound express past the signalbox at Hest Bank, on the West Coast main line north of Lancaster. Note that the water troughs are still *in situ*..

THIS PAGE BOTTOM 50013 *Agincourt* speeds downhill from Hampshire Gap past the site of Amesbury Junction with a Waterloo to Exeter express in May 1984.

THIS PAGE TOP No 50 002 *Superb* rounds the curve at Aller Junction with an express from Penzance to Paddington, augmented with a restaurant car and coaches at Plymouth. This was taken in August 1978, since when the junction has been moved closer to Newton Abbot.

THIS PAGE CENTRE The race is on between a Class 50 in charge of an express from Bristol and a Class 47 on an inter-regional working as they approach Tilehurst in August 1976.

THIS PAGE BOTTOM Approaching Reading with a Penzance–Paddington express in April 1980, No 50 031 *Hood* shows the effect of brake dust on the bodyside. Besides the loss of Class 50s and Mk 2 coaching stock, this location has changed entirely with the rebuilding of the station, its approaches and OHE.

FACING PAGE TOP First sighting of a 'large logo' Class 50. In charge of an Exeter–Waterloo express, No 50 023 *Howe* pulls away from Basingstoke on a sunny day in December 1980.

FACING PAGE BOTTOM No 50 030 accelerates away from a permanent-way slack at Twyford with a Bristol–Paddington express in September 1976. Note the abbreviated locomotive number displayed in the headcode box – a practice adopted by the Western Region with the Class 50s and Class 52s following BR's decision to abandon headcode displays.

TOP Class 50s were not regular traction on the East Coast main line, but following overhaul at Doncaster Works they were used on test runs to and from Newcastle. Here a pristine No 50 010 *Monarch* heads north through Northallerton in June 1981.

CENTRE Its grey roof discoloured by exhaust emissions, a 'large logo' Class 50 climbs away from the Severn Tunnel towards Pilning with an inter-regional express in June 1984.

BOTTOM Dusk is falling at Basingstoke in March 1987 as No 50 006 *Neptune* pauses en route from Waterloo to Exeter. The time exposure has blurred the commuters rushing to get home after a busy day at the office.

TOP For a period of about two years Laira depot rostered Class 50s on Plymouth–Portsmouth/Brighton services, but as Eastleigh depot did not have the facilities to maintain the locomotives, the trains worked extra services to/from Waterloo, providing the opportunity to see Class 50s on the Portsmouth Direct line. No 50 009 *Conqueror* is seen leaving Guildford for Waterloo in September 1987.

CENTRE On a foul day in December 1987 No 50016 *Barham* pulls out of the yard at Blackpool Dries, Burngullow, with a freight for the Drinnick Mill branch.

BOTTOM A Penzance–Plymouth semi-fast draws to a halt at St Germans behind Class 50 No 50 015 *Valiant* in April 1988.

FACING PAGE TOP There can be no doubt where this shot was taken! In charge of a down West of England express, an unidentified Class 52 'Western' is pictured just west of Twyford in March 1974.

FACING PAGE CENTRE Class 52 No 1010 *Western Campaigner* speeds through Taplow in May 1975 with an express from Paddington to the west of England.

FACING PAGE BOTTOM No 1071 *Western Renown* takes the empties back to the Mendips to collect another load of stone for one of the M25 construction sites. This photograph was taken at Ruscombe in May 1975; in October 1987 the infamous hurricane would snap the top off the elm tree in the background.

THIS PAGE TOP An unidentified 'Western' heads an up freight through Bridgend in March 1976. The speakers on the footbridge look large enough to alert the whole of South Wales, let alone this end of the station!

THIS PAGE CENTRE There were two types of locomotive to which BR blue seemed particularly unsuited, these being the Class 52 'Western' and the Class 55 'Deltic'. Looking very drab, with a parcels train to match, No 1051 *Western Ambassador* ambles along the up relief line near Purley-on-Thames in August 1976.

THIS PAGE BOTTOM The 'Westerns' had their yellow ends confined to the cab fronts (rather than being carried around the side windows) and, viewed broadside-on, looked very plain. Illustrating the point is another shot of No 1051 *Western Ambassador*, here working an up express near Ruscombe in September 1976.

CHAPTER 6 TYPE 5s

ABOVE On its regular stamping-ground, 'Deltic' No 55 004 *Queen's Own Highlander* storms away from York
on its way from King's Cross to Newcastle in October 1975.

TOP Very unusual fare on the Western Region at Waltham St Lawrence in October 1975 in the form of 'Deltic' No 55 003 *Meld*, seen heading the return leg of a special from Paddington to Cardiff. In the days before the mobile phone an 'exclusive' was obtained at this location!

CENTRE An Edinburgh–King's Cross express headed by Class 55 'Deltic' No D9017 *Durham Light Infantry* seen just south of Drem in November 1973.

BOTTOM In sunnier conditions in March 1979 No 55 012 *Crepello* approaches Woolmer Green, where the up relief line merges with the up main.

THIS PAGE TOP In charge of a King's Cross–York semi-fast, No 55 017 *Durham Light Infantry* speeds past Langford in August 1980.

THIS PAGE CENTRE An unobstructed view at Marholm in the days before electrification, as 'Deltic' No 55 015 *Tulyar* heads north with a King's Cross–York semi-fast. Note the plaque between the headlights, presented in recognition of the locomotive's participation in the Liverpool & Manchester 150 celebrations held at Rainhill the year before this picture was taken in August 1981.

THIS PAGE BOTTOM Typical of the Yorkshire Coalfield workings is this merry-go-round train destined for either Eggborough or Drax power station. The work-stained Class 56 – one of the early, Romanian-built examples – is about to pass Sudforth Lane crossing in June 1981, at which time substantial construction work was underway at Kellingley Colliery, visible in the background.

FACING PAGE TOP In the late 1970s pairs of Class 56s replaced triple-heading Class 37s on the Port Talbot–Llanwern iron-ore trains. Here No 56 033 and a classmate struggle up the bank at Stormy Down in September 1979.

FACING PAGE BOTTOM Wylye Valley stone traffic is represented by this view of Class 56 No 56 038 *Western Mail* returning empties from Botley to Merehead, passing one of the occupation crossings near Stockton (Wilts) in September 1983.

THIS PAGE TOP In the days when the steel works at Llanwern was still fully operational a pair of Class 56s leave with empty ore carriers for Port Talbot. The second locomotive is No 56 032 *Sir De Morgannwg/County of South Glamorgan*, being readily identifiable on account of its huge nameplates, which must surely have increased axle loadings! The photograph was taken in December 1983.

THIS PAGE CENTRE A train of merry-go-round empties passes Welbeck Colliery Junction in May 1986. The Class 56 locomotive would appear to be in less-than-prime condition, judging from the exhaust.

THIS PAGE BOTTOM Pioneer Class 56 No 56 001 waits patiently at Theale stone terminal in April 1987 whilst its train is unloaded. Note the grab unloading the other rake of wagons.

FACING PAGE TOP No 56 054, with abbreviated number on the front end, heads east at Checker House with a merry-go-round train destined for either West Burton or Cottam power station. The photograph was taken in February 1988.

FACING PAGE BOTTOM The road is set for 'large logo' Class 56 No 56 120 as it passes the derelict signalbox at Norton East Junction in February 1988 with an empty merry-go-round working.

CHAPTER 7 DMUs

ABOVE A very clean Class 101 waits to leave Whitby for Middlesbrough in the drizzle of a June 1981 day.

TOP A unique example of a Class 100 was the 'Stourton Special', used by management for various purposes. In its one-off colour scheme, it is passing Whitwell in July 1987. Note the remains of the station platforms and goods shed.

ABOVE A Class 100 DMU enters Nuneaton station from the south on a Leicester–Birmingham New Street service in March 1982.

THIS PAGE TOP A pair of two-car Class 101s rush across the level crossing at Dilston, on their way from Hexham to Newcastle in June 1983.

THIS PAGE CENTRE Having arrived in its home city in June 1987, Norwich-based Class 101 set No 103 appears in no hurry to move anywhere else for the time being.

THIS PAGE BOTTOM With the steelworks steaming well in the background, a mixed Class 101/108 formation leaves Grangetown en route from Darlington to Saltburn in February 1988.

FACING PAGE TOP With the withdrawal of the Class 117 and 119 units used hitherto, Class 101s were introduced on the Surrey Hills services. Photographed in April 1988 between the chalk tunnels at Guildford, set No L835 was on a Reading–Tonbridge service and although still in BR blue-and-grey had acquired a Network SouthEast logo on the front end.

FACING PAGE BOTTOM Kirton Lime Sidings signalbox stands proud as a Class 101 speeds past on its way from Cleethorpes to Sheffield in April 1988.

THIS PAGE TOP Having posted an on-time (15.48) arrival from Chester, the driver of a Class 103 relaxes as passengers disembark at Crewe in August 1981.

THIS PAGE CENTRE A classic pre-electrification view at King's Cross, recorded in October 1973. With a 'Deltic' resting between duties and a Class 31 acting as station pilot, a Class 105 unit emerges from Gasworks Tunnel and approaches the suburban platforms.

THIS PAGE BOTTOM Scottish Region Class 104 set No 456 comes off the Forth Bridge at Dalmeny on its way to Edinburgh from Dunfermline in March 1988.

FACING PAGE TOP Rock Ferry in August 1981, with a Class 103 arriving on a service from Chester.

FACING PAGE BOTTOM Autumn sunlight picks out the decorative ironwork supporting the station awnings at Kettering, where a Class 104 has arrived from Bletchley in October 1985.

FACING PAGE TOP Edinburgh Waverley in August 1975, with a Class 105 waiting to leave for Cowdenbeath. The open doors emphasise the contours of the bodyside.

FACING PAGE CENTRE In common with a number of first-generation DMU types the Class 105s never gained blue-and-grey livery. On its way from Cambridge to Ipswich in August 1983, Norwich-based set No 54 calls at Stowmarket – one of those stations where so much has changed (as have the cars). And is Gammer's still in business?

FACING PAGE BOTTOM Worked by a three-car Class 107 formation, a service from Glasgow Central terminates at Barrhead in September 1979. The second man looks suitably bored!

THIS PAGE TOP A number of DMUs were painted in a reverse colour scheme following refurbishment in the late 1970s. The photograph shows a Class 108 calling at Kiveton Park on a Sheffield–Cleethorpes working in November 1977.

THIS PAGE CENTRE Class 108s were quite widespread in the Midlands and North of England. In this picture a typical two-car formation is leaving Chester for Helsby in March 1981, when semaphores still abounded.

THIS PAGE BOTTOM Services between Manchester and Chester were also worked by Class 108s. Framed by the station's decorative ironwork, a pair of twin sets depart from Northwich in April 1985. Note also the handsome platform clock (right).

THIS PAGE TOP Another example of a Class 108 duty, as a Barrow–Lancaster train awaits departure from Grange-over-Sands on a grey day in November 1986.

THIS PAGE CENTRE Displaying local set number 261 (barely discernible beneath the driver's window), a Class 108 unit passes the down yard near Beeston as it heads west away from Nottingham in June 1988.

THIS PAGE BOTTOM Formed of a three-car Class 110 unit leading a four-car Class 123, a Hull–Manchester train passes a fine array of semaphore signals at Staddlethorpe in July 1981.

FACING PAGE TOP A Class 110/108 formation passes Bolton Percy on its way to York in June 1988.

FACING PAGE CENTRE The Class 110s were associated primarily with the North of England. By now 'owned' by the newly created Provincial Sector but still in Rail blue and grey, a two-car set on a Sheffield–York service passes through Rotherham Masborough in June 1987. The station was destined to close in October the following year.

FACING PAGE BOTTOM The Class 114s were visually similar to the Class 108s but, being less powerful, were confined to the flat lands of East Anglia. This example was photographed at Sleaford, working a Lincoln–Peterborough service, in March 1986.

TOP This Class 114 unit in reverse livery can scarcely have appealed to passengers, having clearly not seen a washing plant for some time. It is pictured arriving at Elton & Orston in July 1980 on a Grantham–Derby service.

CENTRE A number of Class 114s at Cambridge were converted to take newspapers and parcels. Now adorned with red and yellow stripes, one such unit stands at Cambridge in July 1987, allowing comparison of the plain-blue livery with the blue-and-grey.

BOTTOM The four-car Class 115 units were always associated with the lines from Marylebone. In drab all-blue livery, one heads towards Princes Risborough, where the up line is split from the down so as to ease the grade. The train is a Marylebone–Banbury service, the date May 1975.

TOP A most unusual sight just north of Hatch End on Cup Final day in May 1985 was this pair of Class 115s, by now in the much more attractive blue-and-grey livery, which had headed south an hour or so previously, presumably to Wermbley. A small green Chiltern Line logo can just be discerned on the grey area immediately aft of the cab door.

CENTRE Classes 116, 117 and 118 were visually almost identical. In this picture Western Region Class 116 set No B436 leaves Ledbury en route from Hereford to Worcester in March 1984.

BOTTOM Arriving from Blaenau Ffestiniog, a pair of Class 116s draws into the platform at Llandudno Junction in June 1987.

FACING PAGE TOP Tyseley-allocated Class 116 set No T401 goes over the top of the Lickey Incline at Blackwell en route from Birmingham to Worcester in August 1988. The effect of the gradient is most apparent, while the Malvern Hills can be seen in the far distance.

FACING PAGE CENTRE A sunny spring day in April 1975 facilitated this shot of Class 117 set No L457 passing Waltham St Lawrence on its way from Paddington to Didcot.

FACING PAGE BOTTOM A most unusual train to see at Andover was this Class 117, No L427, which was being used on an Andover–Salisbury shuttle service in association with an open day at Andover in March 1986.

THIS PAGE TOP In the reverse two-tone scheme, Class 118 set No C314 idles away at Rhymney between workings in August 1979. Much as workings out of Paddington were monopolised by the Class 117s, these units were staple fare on the South Wales valley lines.

THIS PAGE CENTRE Class 118 set No C470 enters Barry station on a service from Barry Island in August 1986. Note Cardiff Canton depot's Welsh embellishments.

THIS PAGE BOTTOM A hybrid Class 118/119 set, No C583, reverses at Carmarthen in June 1987 en route from Pembroke to Swansea.

THIS PAGE TOP The Class 119s were regulars on the ex-SECR route from Reading to Redhill and thence to either Tonbridge or Gatwick Airport. This view at Gomshall shows set No L579 on a Tonbridge working in May 1983. The platforms here are staggered, in line with SECR practice.

THIS PAGE CENTRE Class 119 set No L571 about to pass under the slip road off the M3 near Hawley on its way from Reading to Tonbridge in May 1987.

THIS PAGE BOTTOM A sight never recorded before or since was that of a Class 119, set No L584, passing Potbridge in April 1987. There were engineering works on the Reading–Guildford line, and the train is believed to have been a Reading–Gatwick Airport service (a regular '119' working), although Reading–Basingstoke–Woking–Guildford seems a convoluted route to avoid 'bustitution'.

FACING PAGE TOP The signals at Johnstone are set for the Milford Haven line as Class 120 set No C504 approaches in October 1976.

FACING PAGE CENTRE The Class 120s were quite widespread in operation. Here a Crewe–Lincoln train passes the signalbox and crossing at Cresswell in May 1983. Note the signal already reset to Danger.

FACING PAGE BOTTOM A Class 120 arrives at Wrexham General on a Chester–Shrewsbury service in March 1984.

TOP Afternoon sun highlights a Class 120 arriving at Whitchurch en route from Crewe to Shrewsbury in April 1984. The northbound semaphore looks to be well guyed.

CENTRE Working from Oxford to Didcot, Class 121 'Bubble Car' No L128 arrives at Appleford, with its distinctive pagoda shelter, on a sunny day in December 1985. The contents of the fare box seem unlikely to be bolstered!

BOTTOM Class 121 No P109 awaits custom at Liskeard on a wet day in December 1987. Anyone for Looe?

LEFT Operating the Stockport–Stalybridge service, a Class 121, departs Guide Bridge on a typically wet afternoon in April 1986.

RIGHT The Swindon-built Class 123 'Inter-City' units were normally confined to Western Region services in the 1960s and '70s, so what this nine-car formation was doing heading down the Southampton main line at Battledown in May 1974 is anybody's guess.

BELOW By the time this photograph was taken in March 1983 the Class 123s had all been transferred to the Eastern Region at Hull. Now adorned with Trans-Pennine branding, a four-car set was recorded at one of the bay platforms at Leeds. Note that the headcode boxes have been removed.

ABOVE The Class 124 'Trans-Pennine' units never wandered from their designated routes on the Leeds–Manchester corridor. Here one of the five-car sets approaches Manchester Victoria on its way from Hull to Liverpool in June 1974.

TOP The Class 124 were perhaps the best-looking of all DMUs. Here a four-car train pauses at Leeds *en route* from Liverpool to Hull in March 1983.

CENTRE The Class 126 design was similar to the Class 120 but was equipped at one end with a corridor connection as well as a small driving cab. One of these three-car units is seen at Elderslie Junction, leading a Glasgow Central–Stranraer train. In September 1979, when the photograph was taken, the junction and semaphores were still in situ, and the one-time Hillman Imp factory at Linwood was still in production – even if the cars were seemingly available only in red or white!

BOTTOM Noteworthy through having hydraulic (rather than mechanical) transmission, the Class 127 units were used on suburban services from St Pancras and Moorgate. One is seen north of Radlett on a Bedford service in March 1979, two years before the wires went up.

TOP By November 1981 electrification wires had been erected, but Bedford services were still in the hands of Class 127s, pending trade-union acceptance of the new Class 317 electric units. A St Pancras-bound train is seen near Millbrook.

CENTRE The Class 128s were designed for parcels traffic and would often tow unpowered vans, as seen in this view of an up train at Lower Basildon in August 1975.

BOTTOM One Derby Lightweight DMU was converted for use as an ultrasonic test train. It is seen at Oldbury in October 1975, heading in the direction of Wolverhampton.

CHAPTER 8 DEMUs

ABOVE Looking quite smart, albeit in unrelieved blue, 'Hampshire' Class 205 No 1124 accelerates (perhaps not the best word to choose for these units) away from Basingstoke on a sunny day in December 1980, on its way from Reading to Portsmouth Harbour.

TOP Seen approaching Polhill Tunnel, Class 202 No 1016 brings up the rear of a Hastings–Charing Cross express. The date is March 1986, and on the hillside work is in progress on construction of the M25.

CENTRE Barely visible in between two Class 201 power cars from set No 1003 is a high-speed test coach. The unusual formation was photographed heading south at Swaythling in May 1985.

BOTTOM The diesel-electric multiple-units of Classes 201, 202 and 203 were allocated to the Hastings line, when it was still double-track through the limited-clearance tunnels. On a service from Charing Cross to Hastings, Class 201 No 1006 passes Chislehurst in March 1980.

THIS PAGE TOP One for the track-bashers, some of whom were distinctly peeved that the unit was rostered the wrong way around, with the power car at the front! Class 205 No 1110 is seen on the remains of the Tidworth line at Ludgershall as part of a Branch Line Society trip on a foggy day in March 1986.

THIS PAGE CENTRE Formed in the late 1970s, the Class 204s were similar to the '205s', but the centre coach was a former driving trailer with a cab (now redundant) at one end. No 1402 departs the Brunel-designed station at Mortimer in January 1983 on a Reading–Portsmouth working.

THIS PAGE BOTTOM Photographed in May 1988 from an overbridge that has since been removed, Class 205 No 205 028 is seen between the loops and the tunnel at Wallers Ash, on a Reading–Portsmouth working.

FACING PAGE TOP Employed almost exclusively on Reading–Tonbridge workings, the Class 206 units were known as 'Tadpoles', owing to the combination of two narrow-bodied 'Hastings' coaches and a full-width driving trailer. In the original plain-blue livery, No 1206 waits to depart Guilford for Reading in August 1975.

FACING PAGE BOTTOM By the summer of 1979 the narrow 'Hastings' coaches of the Class 206 units had been repainted blue and grey, but the driving trailers remained plain blue. Presumably this was because the 'Hastings' coaches were considered main-line stock, whereas the 'Hampshire' cars were regarded as suburban stock, which in the late 1970s was still being turned out in plain blue; the fact that the Class 206s were not repainted in a uniform livery demonstrates that they were only ever intended as a stop-gap. Illustrating the anomaly, No 1203 leaves Wokingham on its way from Reading to Tonbridge in August 1979.

TOP Bound for Tonbridge, 'Tadpole' No 1204 shows the mixed colours quite clearly at Reigate in July 1979. *Harry Luff*

ABOVE The Oxted-line units of Class 207 were only occasionally used on the ex-SECR line to Reading, but here, in August 1979, No 1317 is waiting to leave the then Platform 4 for Tonbridge. The photograph was taken from the site of the old Reading South station, by now in use as a car park. The cars certainly bring back a few memories!

TOP An unusual London Bridge–Eastbourne working approaches Gatwick Airport in March 1986. Class 207 No 1301 brings up the rear of the nine-car formation.

ABOVE The two Class 210 units were prototypes built to an over-generous specification that was not perpetuated. Having settled down to regular use on local trains from Reading, No 210 001 (the four-car unit, No 210 002 being three-car) leaves Newbury Racecourse on a stopping service to Bedwyn in July 1986.

CHAPTER 9 'BLUE PULLMANS' AND HIGH SPEED TRAINS

TOP The 'Blue Pullman' units were not given a TOPS class number. In this view, a service from Paddington to Wolverhampton is seen near Solihull in July 1965. *Michael Mensing*

CENTRE The 'Blue Pullmans' kept to their Birmingham-, Bristol- and Manchester-line diagrams, with little variation, except when rostered for special services. Seen east of Beechwood Tunnel in March 1966, this set has been hired to work a Rugby League special from Coventry to Liverpool. *Michael Mensing*

BOTTOM The High Speed Train was arguably the spiritual successor to the 'Blue Pullmans', and indeed the prototype was turned out in a reversed livery similar to that applied latterly to Pullman stock. Photographed on its first day of trial running on the Western Region in May 1975, it is seen at Ruscombe on the return working from Paddington to Bristol. Although the unit was officially Class 252, the two power cars were described in some circles as Class 41, reusing the classification applied first to the five A1A-A1A 'Warships' (see page 42).

LEFT The production HSTs of Classes 253 (Western Region) and 254 (Eastern) entered service from 1976, power car No 43012 being seen bringing up the rear of a down train approaching Ruscombe in September of that year. The photograph shows to good advantage the striking livery applied to the power cars; the Mk 3 coaches were turned out in standard blue-and-grey. The white streak in the sky above the corridor connection is not a blemish but a Concorde climbing noisily away from Heathrow!

TOP HST set No 253 003 leaves the cutting at Pangbourne as it speeds past on its way to Paddington in September 1976. The application of set numbers was soon discontinued as power cars came in for servicing and became separated from their original sets; indeed, for a short time power cars could be observed side by side on different trains but bearing the same number, making a mockery of the system.

ABOVE Initially given 254 xxx unit numbers, the Eastern Region HSTs comprised eight coaches, the WR sets having seven. A Newcastle–King's Cross train, complete with a pair of restaurant/kitchen cars, is seen near Otterington in June 1981. Although, as here, the physical application of set numbers was soon abandoned, in the Rail-blue era the HSTs were always known as Class 253 or 254 units; more recently it has become common practice to refer to the power cars as Class 43, reprising the code used previously for NBL-built B-B 'Warships' (see page 43).